MW01182045

ISBN: 979-8-5555-7271-4

www.sovereigngrace.com

Designed and Typeset by: Jordan Daniel Singer

WE BELIEVE

A Statement of Faith

SOVEREIGN GRACE
CHURCHES

CONTENTS OF
THE STATEMENT OF FAITH

THE PERSON OF JESUS CHRIST

THE SAVING WORK OF JESUS CHRIST

THE PERSON AND WORK OF THE HOLY SPIRIT

THE GOSPEL AND THE APPLICATION OF SALVATION BY THE HOLY SPIRIT

THE EMPOWERING MINISTRY OF THE SPIRIT

LIFE IN CHRIST

THE CHURCH OF CHRIST

THE LAST THINGS

THE SCRIPTURES

God and Revelation

Our eternal, transcendent, all-glorious God, who forever exists as Father, Son, and Holy Spirit, is by his very nature a communicative being.[1] He both creates[2] and governs[3] through his words and has graciously revealed himself[4] to humanity[5] in order to commune with us.[6] He has revealed himself through creation and providence in ways plain to all people, leaving no one without a testimony of himself.[7] He also revealed himself through specific words, that we might come to a fuller knowledge of his character and will,[8] learning what is necessary for salvation and life.[9] Through the medium of human language,[10] which is suitable and adequate for communication with those who bear his

---

1. Gen 1:3; John 1:1; 17:5; Heb 3:7.
2. Gen 1; Ps 33:9; 147:18; 148:5; Col 1:15-17; Heb 11:3.
3. Ps 29; Lam 3:37-38; Isa 46:8-11; Col 1:15-17; Heb 1:3.
4. Deut 29:29; 1 Sam 3:21.
5. Gen 1:26; Gen 2:15-17.
6. Acts 17:24-27.
7. Gen 3:8-9; Ps 19:1-6; Hos 2:20; John 10:14-15; Acts 14:17; Rom 1:19-21.
8. Ps 19:7-11.
9. 2 Tim 3:15-17; 2 Pet 1:3-4.
10. Exod 32:16; Heb 1:1-2.

image, God has preserved in Holy Scripture the only authoritative and complete revelation for all humanity.[11]

The Origin of Scripture

All of Scripture is breathed out by God,[12] being accurately delivered through various human authors by the inspiration and sovereign agency of the Holy Spirit.[13] We therefore receive the sixty-six books of the Old and New Testaments as the perfect, infallible, and authoritative Word of God. With the fullness of revelation given in Christ and his completed redemptive work, no new normative revelation will or need be given until Christ returns.[14] In its original manuscripts, the whole of Scripture (and all its parts) is inerrant—without error in all it affirms.[15] Because there is one divine author behind all of Scripture, we are able to arrive confidently at a harmonious, doctrinally unified understanding of the whole. Furthermore, God in his loving providence has determined to preserve his Word as pure and trustworthy throughout history,[16] just as he guided the early church in discerning and identifying the canon of Scripture he inspired.

The Attributes of Scripture

Believers live by every word that comes from the mouth of God.[17] The Word of God is therefore necessary and

---

11. Rev 22:18-19.
12. 2 Tim 3:16; 1 Thess 2:13.
13. 2 Pet 1:19-21.
14. Heb 1:1-2; Rev 22:18-19.
15. Ps 119:160; Prov 30:5-6; John 10:35.
16. Ps 12:6-7; Mark 13:31.
17. Matt 4:4.

wholly sufficient for knowing the Father's love in Christ, experiencing his glorious plan of redemption, and being instructed in the way of fruitful and godly living.[18] The Word of God is clear, and everything we need in order to know, love, and fellowship with God can be plainly understood through ordinary means, without appeal to any human authority.[19] Although not all Scripture is equally plain, when its intended meaning is misunderstood, the fault lies not in the clarity of God's communication but in the recipient.[20] Scripture alone is our supreme and final authority and the rule of faith and life. The Scriptures must not be added to or taken away from, and all creeds, confessions, teachings, and prophecies are to be tested by the final authority of God's Word.[21]

The Reception of Scripture

We come to know that the Bible is God's Word through Scripture's own self-attesting authority[22] and by the work of the Holy Spirit bearing witness through the Word in our hearts.[23] As the Scriptures are preached and read,[24] the Spirit delights to illuminate our minds so that we understand, cherish, and obey his Word.[25] God's intended meaning is revealed through the intentions of the inspired human authors, rendering the truth of God's Word a fixed, historical reality. Therefore, the Bible is to be prayerfully interpreted according to its context and original intent,

18. Rom 10:13-17; 2 Tim 3:15-17.

19. Deut 30:11-14; Ps 19:7; 119:130; Acts 17:1.

20. Luke 24:25; John 8:43.

21. Rev 22:18-19.

22. 2 Pet 1:17-19; Luke 16:29-31; Heb 4:12-13.

23. 1 Cor 2:14; 2 Cor 3:14-16; Ps 119:18, 27, 34, 73.

24. 1 Tim 4:13; 2 Tim 4:1-2.

25. Ps 19:7-11; James 1:22-25.

with due regard to the progressive nature of revelation and the collective interpretation of believers through the ages.[26] Ultimately, Scripture interprets Scripture, and the meaning of each text must be understood in light of the whole. As we devote ourselves to God's Word,[27] we commune with God himself and are fortified in faith, sanctified from sin, strengthened in weakness, and sustained in suffering by his unchanging revelation in Scripture.[28]

26. 2 Tim 2:15.
27. Deut 6:6-7; Ps 1:1-2; 119:1; Josh 1:8.
28. Isa 50:4; 55:10-11; Jer 23:29; John 17:17; Acts 20:32; Rom 15:4; 1 Thess 2:13;
    Heb 4:12.

THE TRIUNE GOD

The Nature of God

There is only one[29] true and living God,[30] who is infinite in being,[31] power,[32] and perfections.[33] God is eternal,[34] independent, and self-sufficient, having life in himself with no need for anyone or anything.[35] He is spirit,[36] transcendent and invisible,[37] with no limitations or imperfections,[38] immutable,[39] and everywhere present with the fullness of his being.[40] His knowledge is exhaustive, including all things actual and possible, so that nothing—past, present, or future—is hidden from his sight.[41] God is not divided into parts, but his whole being includes all of his attributes: he

---

29. Deut 6:4; 1 Cor 8:4-6; 1 Tim 1:17.
30. Jer 10:10; John 17:3; 1 Thess 1:9.
31. Exod 3:14; Job 11:7-9.
32. Ps 24:8; Matt 19:26.
33. Matt 5:48.
34. Ps 90:2; Rev 1:8.
35. Ps 50:10-12; 102:25-27; Acts 17:24-25.
36. John 4:24.
37. Rom 1:20.
38. Ps 18:30.
39. Mal 3:6; James 1:17.
40. Jer 23:23-24; Ps 139:7-10.
41. Isa 42:8; 1 John 3:20.

is entirely holy,[42] loving,[43] wise,[44] just,[45] good,[46] merciful,[47] gracious,[48] and truthful.[49] Our God is the infinite fountain of being[50] who created all things,[51] and all things exist by him and for him.[52] He is supremely powerful to perform all his holy and perfect will, ruling over his creation with total dominion,[53] righteousness,[54] wisdom,[55] and love.[56] In his transcendence, God is incomprehensible in his being and actions, yet he reveals himself such that we can know him truly and personally.[57]

The Holy Trinity

The one true God eternally exists as three persons—Father,[58] Son,[59] and Holy Spirit[60]—infinitely excellent and all-glorious. Each person is fully God, sharing the same deity, attributes, and essential nature, yet there is but one God.[61] Each person is distinct, yet God is not by this distinction divided into three parts, natures, or gods. The Father has always existed as Father, the unbegotten fountain

---

42. Ps 99:9; Rev 15:4.
43. 1 John 4:8.
44. Ps 104:24; Rom 16:27.
45. Deut 32:4; Rom 3:25-26.
46. Ps 106:1; Luke 18:19.
47. Exod 34:6; 2 Cor 1:3.
48. Ps 103:8; 1 Pet 5:10.
49. Ps 12:6; Prov 30:5; Titus 1:2.
50. Ps 36:9; John 5:26.
51. Gen 1:1; Ps 33:6, 9; John 1:3.
52. Rom 11:36; Col 1:16.
53. Ps 115:3; 66:7.
54. Ps 9:8; 36:6.
55. Ps 104:24; Rom 16:27.
56. Exod 34:6; Ps 119:64.
57. Ps 145:3; 1 Cor 2:10-12; Rom 11:33; Col 1:10; Jer 9:23-24.
58. John 6:27; Titus 1:4.
59. John 1:1; 8:58; Col 2:9.
60. Heb 9:14; 1 Cor 3:16; Acts 5:3-4.
61. Deut 6:4; Isa 45:21-22.

of all life.[62] The Son has always existed as Son, eternally begotten of the Father, uncreated and without beginning, of one essence with the Father.[63] The Holy Spirit has always existed as Spirit, eternally proceeding from the Father and the Son, and of one essence with them.[64] The Godhead thus exists in a perfect unity, indivisible as to nature and substance, yet inseparably distinguished as persons who enjoy a fullness of fellowship and love.[65]

The Relations and Actions of the Trinity

The persons of the Trinity, being one in nature, are also inseparably united in their external works,[66] such that to deal with one person is to deal with the Trinity as a whole.[67] Yet within this unity there are distinctions in the way the divine persons relate to each other and to creation,[68] although there is no difference in essence or attributes. Within the Godhead, the ordered relations among the persons are eternal yet without any inequality. In the works of creation, providence, and redemption, the persons fulfill roles consistent with their eternal relations: the Father originates, the Son accomplishes, and the Spirit completes.[69] Nevertheless, the three, thus distinct, are neither divided nor mixed, are of one and the same essence, are equal from all eternity, and are worthy to be worshipped as the one God—Father, Son, and Holy Spirit.[70] *Kind of like: I am a woman, a mother, daughter, and a helper to others. We are a model of the Trinity.*

62. Rom 11:36; Eph 4:6.
63. John 1:1-4; 10:30; Heb 1:3, 5.
64. John 15:26; Gal 4:6.
65. John 3:35; 14:31; 17:24.
66. Gen 1:2; John 1:3; 5:19.
67. John 10:38; 14:9-11.
68. Gen 1:1, 2; Heb 1:2.
69. John 3:16; 6:38; 15:26; Rom 8:13; Gal 4:4; Heb 10:5-7.
70. Rev 5:12-14.

GOD'S SOVEREIGN PURPOSES

God Ordains All Things for His Glory

From all eternity, God sovereignly ordained all that exists and all that occurs in his creation,[71] in order to display the fullness of his glory.[72] God's plans are efficacious, always coming to pass,[73] and they are universal, encompassing all the affairs of nature,[74] history,[75] and individual lives.[76] These decrees are an exercise of his free,[77] unchangeable,[78] wise,[79] and holy will.[80] Yet God, in his foreordination, is not the author of sin,[81] nor do his decrees negate the will of his creatures, who act with the power of willing choice in accord with their nature.[82] His ordaining and

---

71. Ps 33:11; Isa 37:26; Eph 1:11.
72. Rom 11:36; Exod 14:17-18; Ps 19:1.
73. Ps 33:11; Isa 46:9-10; 55:11.
74. Job 37:6-13; Col 1:16-17.
75. Ps 33:10-11; Prov 21:1.
76. Prov 16:9; 20:24; Ps 139:6.
77. Rom 9:15.
78. Num 23:19; Heb 6:17.
79. Rom 11:33.
80. Eph 1:11.
81. James 1:13; 1 John 1:5.
82. Acts 2:23; Rom 9:14-24; Phil 2:12-13.

governing all things is compatible with his creatures' moral accountability[83] such that God never condemns a person unjustly.[84] Therefore, all persons are responsible for their actions, which have real and eternal consequences.[85]

God's Grace in Election

God in his great love, before the foundation of the world, chose those whom he would save in Christ Jesus.[86] God's election is entirely gracious[87] and not at all conditioned upon foreseen faith, obedience, perseverance, or any merit in those whom God has chosen.[88] His decision to set his saving love on the elect is based entirely on his sovereign will and good pleasure.[89] The number of God's elect is fixed for eternity, and no one who has been chosen by God will be lost.[90] In the mystery of his will, God passes over the non-elect,[91] withholding his mercy and punishing them for their sins as a display of his holy justice and wrath.[92]

As God has appointed the elect to glory,[93] so has he foreordained all the means necessary to carry out his saving purposes.[94] Those whom he has predestined are redeemed by Christ,[95] effectually called to faith by his Spirit, justified,

83. Rom 3:19.
84. Dan 4:37; Rom 1:20.
85. Luke 10:28; John 3:16.
86. Acts 13:48; Eph 1:4-5; 2 Tim 1:9.
87. Eph 1:6; 2:8-9; Rom 11:5-8.
88. Rom 9:11-18; 1 Cor 1:26-31.
89. 2 Tim 1:9.
90. John 10:25-29; Rom 8:29-30; 11:5-8.
91. Rom 9:17-22; Jude 4; Rev 20:15.
92. Rom 9:22; Rev 19:1-5.
93. Col 3:4; Rom 8:29-30.
94. Rom 9:22; Rev 19:1-5.
95. 1 Thess 5:9-10; Titus 2:14.

adopted, sanctified,[96] and kept by God's power to the end.[97] God does all of this in order to demonstrate his mercy to the praise of his glorious grace.[98]

Although attended with mystery, the doctrine of election should not produce speculation, introspection, apathy, or pride[99] but rather humility, gratitude, assurance, evangelistic passion, and eternal praise for the undeserved grace of God in Christ.[100]

96. Rom 8:30; Eph 1:5; 2 Thess 2:13.

97. 1 Pet 1:5.

98. Eph 1:6, 12, 14.

99. Deut 29:29; Ps 131:1; Rom 9:20.

100. 1 Cor 1:26-31; Eph 1:5-6, 12; 1 Thess 1:2, 4; 2 Thess 2:13; 2 Tim 2:10.

CREATION, PROVIDENCE, AND MAN

God Creates and Rules All Things

In the beginning, the triune God freely created out of nothing the universe and everything in it by the word of his power, all for his own pleasure and the display of his glory.[101] God declared the entirety of his creation to be very good,[102] and even in its fallen state it tells of his greatness[103] and is to be delighted in[104] and stewarded for his glory.[105] As supreme Creator, God is separate from and transcendent over all he has made.[106] As sovereign Lord, he is present with his creation to sustain all things,[107] govern all creatures, and direct all circumstances in accord with his holy and loving will.[108] In everything God supremely acts

---

101. Gen 1; Ps 19:1; 33:6; John 1:3; Col 1:15-17; Heb 11:3; Rev 4:11.
102. Gen 1:31.
103. Ps 19:1-6; Rom 1:20.
104. Ps 111:2; 1 Tim 4:4.
105. Gen 1:26, 28; Ps 8.
106. 1 Kings 8:27; Isa 6:1; 66:1.
107. Ps 145:15; 147:8-9; Luke 12:24; Heb 1:3.
108. Eph 1:11; Rom 8:28-29.

for his glory[109] and for the good of his people in Christ,[110] granting us great comfort and unshakable hope in God's love, wisdom, and faithfulness to us in this life and in eternity.[111]

Man's Creation in God's Image

God created man, male and female,[112] in his own image[113] as the crown of creation and the object of his special care.[114] God directly created Adam from the dust of the earth,[115] and Eve from Adam's side,[116] as the parents of the entire human race.[117] They were created to know and glorify their Maker by trusting in his goodness and obeying his word.[118] God gave them dominion over all creation, to fill, subdue, and steward the earth as his representatives.[119] All human beings are likewise made in the image of God.[120] Despite the effects of the fall on sinful humanity,[121] all people remain God's image bearers, capable of fellowship with him and possessing intrinsic dignity and value at every stage of life from conception to death.[122] Redemption in Christ progressively restores fallen men and women to their true humanity as they are conformed to the image of Christ.[123]

---

109. Isa 43:7; Eph 1:6, 12.
110. Gen 50:20; Rom 8:28; Eph 1:22.
111. Rom 5:3-5; 8:31; Phil 1:6; 1 Pet 4:19; Jude 24.
112. Gen 1:27.
113. Gen 1:26-27; 9:6.
114. Ps 8:4-8.
115. Gen 2:7.
116. Gen 2:22.
117. 1 Cor 15:22, 45-49.
118. Gen 2:16-17; Eccles 3:11; Isa 43:7; Rom 1:19-21.
119. Gen 1:26, 28.
120. Gen 9:6; James 3:9.
121. Rom 3:23; Eph 2:1; 4:18; Col 1:21.
122. Ps 139:13-16; Jer 1:5; Rom 14:8; James 3:9.
123. Rom 8:29; 2 Cor 3:18; Eph 4:24; Col 3:10.

Man as Male and Female

Men and women are both made in the image of God and are equal before him in dignity and worth.[124] Gender, designated by God through our biological sex, is therefore neither incidental to our identity nor fluid in its definition, but is essential to our identity as male and female. Although the fall distorts and damages God's design for gender and its expression,[125] these remain part of the beauty of God's created order. Men and women reflect and represent God in distinct and complementary ways, and these differences are to be honored and celebrated in all dimensions of life. To deny or seek to remove these differences is to distort a fundamental way in which we glorify God as male and female.

Marriage, Sexuality, and Singleness

Biblical manhood and womanhood enrich human flourishing in all its dimensions. God instituted marriage as the union of one man and one woman who complement each other in a one-flesh union[126] that ultimately serves as a type of the union between Christ and his church.[127] This remains the only normative pattern of sexual relations for humanity. Husbands are to exercise headship sacrificially and with humility,[128] and wives are to serve as helpers to their husbands, willingly supporting and submitting to their leadership.[129] Together these complementary roles bring joy

---

124. Gen 1:27; 9:6; Gal 3:28; James 3:9.

125. Gen 3:16-19.

126. Gen 2:18-25.

127. Eph 5:31-33.

128. Eph 5:25-30; Col 3:19; 1 Pet 3:7.

129. Gen 2:18; Eph 5:22-24; Col 3:18; 1 Pet 3:1-2.

and blessing to each other and display the beauty of God's purposes to the world. Single men and women are no less able to enjoy and honor God and no less important to his purposes. They also are to give expression to God's image in distinct and complementary ways, flourishing as his image bearers and bringing him glory in their singleness.[130]

130. E.g., 1 Cor 7:6-8; Luke 2:36-37

MAN'S SIN
AND ITS EFFECTS

The Origin of Sin

God originally created man innocent and righteous, without stain or corruption.[131] In this state, Adam and Eve enjoyed a fullness of life in communion with God, delighting in him and his righteous will yet capable of transgressing.[132] Despite these privileges, they were led astray by Satan[133] and willfully sinned against their Creator by doing what he had forbidden.[134] In their rebellion they doubted his character, rejected his authority, and disobeyed his word.[135] Man's trespass of God's command[136] brought enmity with God[137] and the curse of death.[138] Because God had established Adam as the representative head of the human race,[139] his sin was imputed to all his descendants, bringing guilt, condemnation,

---

131. Gen 1:27, 31; Eccles 7:29.
132. Gen 2:7-9, 15-17.
133. Gen 3:13; 2 Cor 11:3.
134. Gen 3:6-7.
135. Gen 2:17; 3:1-6.
136. Gen 3:17; Rom 5:18-19.
137. Gen 3:8-10; Isa 59:2.
138. Gen 2:16-17; Rom 5:12.
139. Rom 5:12-19; 1 Cor 15:22, 49.

and death to humanity.[140] Therefore, we are all by nature corrupt[141] and inclined to evil from conception.[142]

The Effects of Sin

From the inherited corruption of humanity[143] arise all the sins that we commit.[144] All people are now by nature enemies of God,[145] living under the power of Satan,[146] subject to the curse of the law,[147] and deserving of eternal punishment.[148] Moreover, the whole nature of man has been corrupted by the fall, and no part of man is untainted by sin.[149] Although fallen people remain in the image of God[150] and manifest the virtues of common grace, they are incapable of pleasing God,[151] meriting his favor,[152] or freeing themselves from their bondage to sin.[153] Their hearts are hardened,[154] their understanding is darkened,[155] their consciences are corrupted,[156] their spiritual sight is blinded,[157] and their deeds are evil.[158] Therefore, all people are dead in sin and without hope apart from salvation in Jesus Christ.[159]

---

140. 1 Cor 15:21-22; Rom 5:12-18.
141. Gen 6:5; Job 14:4; 15:14; Jer 17:9; Eph 2:3.
142. Ps 51:5; Gen 8:21; Rom 3:23.
143. Rom 5:12; Eph 2:3.
144. Ps 14:3; 51:1-5; 58:3; James 1:14; Matt 15:19.
145. Eph 2:3; Rom 5:10; 8:7.
146. John 8:44; Acts 26:18; 2 Tim 2:26; 2 Cor 4:4; 1 John 5:19; Eph 2:2.
147. Gal 3:10; Rom 4:15; Deut 28:45.
148. Dan 12:2; Matt 25:46; Rev 20:14-15; Rom 1:32; 6:32.
149. Gen 6:5; Rom 3:10-18; 7:18; Eph 2:3; Jer 17:9.
150. Gen 9:6; James 3:9.
151. Rom 8:8; Heb 11:6.
152. Isa 64:6; Rom 3:20; Gal 2:16.
153. John 8:34; Eph 2:1-2.
154. Eph 4:18; Matt 13:15.
155. Rom 1:18-23, 28; Eph 4:18.
156. Titus 1:15; 1 Tim 4:2.
157. 2 Cor 4:4; John 9:39; Rom 11:8.
158. Isa 64:6; John 3:19; Col 1:21.
159. Eph 2:12-13.

The curse of the fall corrupted not only mankind but the entire created order, subjecting the world to futility, decay, and death.[160] Both the cursed creation and moral evil produce calamity, suffering, hostility, and injustice in the world.[161] The groaning of the created order reminds us of our fallenness and causes us to long for the redemption of all things under Christ.[162]

---

160. Gen 3:14-19; Rom 8:19-25.

161. Eccles 4:1; Matt 24:7; John 16:33; Titus 3:3.

162. Rom 8:22-23; 1 Cor 15:24-25; Heb 2:8; Rev 21:4.

THE PERSON
OF JESUS CHRIST

Incarnation and Two Natures

In the fullness of time God the Father sent his eternal Son,[163] the second person of the Trinity,[164] into the world as Jesus the Christ.[165] He was conceived by the Holy Spirit[166] and born of the virgin Mary,[167] taking on himself a fully human nature with all its attributes and frailties, yet without sin.[168] In this union, two whole, perfect, and distinct natures were inseparably joined together in the one person of the divine Son without confusion, mixture, or change. Our Redeemer acted in and through both his human and divine natures,[169] in ways appropriate to each, with both natures being preserved and neither diminished by the other. Yet both his human and divine natures are united and find expression in the one person of the eternal Son.[170] Thus

---

163. John 3:16; Gal 4:4.
164. John 1:1-2; Heb 1:3.
165. Matt 1:21.
166. Luke 1:35.
167. Matt 1:23; Luke 1:34.
168. John 1:14; Heb 2:16-17; 4:15.
169. Mark 4:35-41; 11:12; Luke 2:52; 6:6-10.
170. John 1:14; Heb 1:1-3.

our Lord Jesus Christ, God the Son incarnate, is fully God and fully man, able to be our all-sufficient savior and the only mediator between God and man.[171]

Earthly Life and Ministry

As God's incarnate Son, our Lord Jesus Christ inaugurated the kingdom of God,[172] fulfilling God's saving purposes[173] and all Old Testament prophecies about the One to come:[174] he is the Seed of the woman,[175] the Seed of Abraham,[176] the Prophet like Moses,[177] the Priest after the order of Melchizedek,[178] the Son of David,[179] the Suffering Servant,[180] and God's appointed Messiah.[181] As such he was anointed by the Holy Spirit[182] and lived a sinless life[183] in complete obedience to his Father.[184] Jesus entered into full human existence, enduring the common infirmities, temptations, and sufferings of mankind. He perfectly revealed the character of God,[185] taught with divine authority and utter truthfulness,[186] extended God's love and compassion,[187]

171. Acts 4:12; 1 Tim 2:5.
172. Mark 1:15; Matt 12:28.
173. Isa 53; Acts 4:12; Rom 3:21-22; 2 Cor 1:20.
174. Luke 24:44; John 5:39.
175. Gen 3:15; Rom 16:20.
176. Gen 15:18; 17:8; Matt 1:1, Gal 3:16.
177. Deut 18:15; Acts 3:22-26.
178. Ps 110:4; Heb 5:5-6.
179. 2 Sam 7:16; Matt 1:1; 22:42-45.
180. Isa 53:3-6; Mark 10:45.
181. Dan 9:25-26; Matt 16:16.
182. Matt 3:16.
183. Heb 2:16-17; 4:15.
184. John 5:19; Phil 2:8.
185. John 1:14, 18; 14:9-11; Heb 1:1-3.
186. Mark 1:22; John 12:49-50; 14:10-11.
187. Matt 9:36; Mark 6:34; John 13:1, 34; 14:21.

and demonstrated his lordship through the working of miracles[188] and the exercise of divine prerogatives.[189]

Death, Resurrection, and Reign

Having fully obeyed his Father in life, our Savior was also obedient unto death.[190] He was crucified under Pontius Pilate, dying a substitutionary death for the sins of his people.[191] He was buried and arose bodily from the dead on the third day,[192] vindicating his identity and saving work as God's Messiah[193] and guaranteeing the defeat of death, our future resurrection, and the glorification of our physical bodies.[194] Forty days later Jesus ascended bodily to heaven,[195] where he is now enthroned at the right hand of God,[196] reigning over all things,[197] and interceding for his people as their Great High Priest.[198] One day he will return to judge all people and angels,[199] putting all his enemies under his feet and dwelling with his people forever.[200]

---

188. See, e.g., Matt 8:1-17; Mark 2:1-12; Luke 7:11-17; John 2:1-11.

189. Matt 11:27; Mark 2:5-12; John 9:39; 10:9, 11; 20:28-29.

190. Phil 2:6-7.

191. Isa 53:5-12; 2 Cor 5:21; Rom 3:24-25; 1 Pet 3:18.

192. Matt 28:1-10; Mark 16:1-18; Luke 24:1-12; John 20:1-10; 1 Cor 15:3-4.

193. Acts 2:32-33; 4:10; 13:32-39; 17:31; Rom 1:3-4; 4:25.

194. 1 Cor 15:20-57.

195. Luke 24:50-53; Acts 1:9.

196. Acts 2:33; 5:31; 7:55-56; Rom 8:34; Eph 1:20; Heb 1:3; 8:1; 10:12.

197. Matt 28:18; John 17:2; Heb 1:3.

198. Heb 4:14; 7:25; 10:21.

199. Matt 25:31-32; Rom 2:16; 2 Tim 4:1.

200. 1 Cor 15:25-27; Heb 2:8.

THE SAVING WORK
OF JESUS CHRIST

The Humiliation of Christ in His Saving Work

In the entirety of his life and death, Jesus Christ humbled himself[201] to serve as our mediator[202] in obedience to his Father's saving purposes.[203] As the second Adam,[204] his sinless life[205] of wholehearted obedience to God's law obtained the gift of perfect righteousness[206] and eternal life[207] for all of God's elect.[208] In his substitutionary death on behalf of his people,[209] Christ offered himself by the Spirit[210] as a perfect sacrifice, which satisfied the demands of God's law by paying the full penalty for their sins.[211] On

---

201. Phil 2:6-8.
202. 1 Tim 2:5; Heb 9:15; 12:24.
203. John 4:34; 5:30; 6:38.
204. Rom 5:14; 1 Cor 15:45.
205. 2 Cor 5:21; Heb 4:15; 1 Pet 2:22.
206. Rom 5:17-21; 2 Cor 5:21; Phil 3:9.
207. John 3:14-16; 5:24; Titus 3:7; 1 John 5:11.
208. John 6:37; 10:29; Eph 1:3-5.
209. Isa 53:4-6, 12; Matt 20:28; 2 Cor 5:21.
210. Heb 9:14.
211. John 19:30; Rom 8:1; Heb 1:3.

the cross, Christ bore our sins,[212] took our punishment,[213] propitiated God's wrath against us,[214] vindicated God's righteousness,[215] and purchased our redemption[216] in order that we might be reconciled to God[217] and live with him in blessed fellowship forever.[218]

The Efficacy of Christ's Saving Work

God the Father was pleased to accept Christ's sacrifice as a complete atonement for sin, raising him to new life[219] and vindicating his identity and work as the Messiah.[220] For those who place their faith in Jesus Christ, God's righteousness requires no further sacrifice for sin,[221] nor is there any human achievement or merit to be added to Christ's accomplishment.[222] The atoning work of Christ is wholly efficacious,[223] securing the full salvation of all the elect by purchasing the forgiveness of sins,[224] the gifts of faith and repentance,[225] eternal life,[226] and every other blessing that comes to God's people.[227] As the sole and sufficient atonement for sin,[228] Christ's saving work is to be proclaimed to all people without exception as the only

212. 1 Pet 2:24.
213. Gal 3:13.
214. Rom 5:9.
215. Rom 3:25-26.
216. Rom 3:24; Eph 1:7.
217. Rom 5:10; 2 Cor 5:18; Col 1:22.
218. Ezek 37:27; John 17:3; Rev 21:3.
219. Acts 3:15; 13:30; Rom 10:9; 1 Cor 15:15.
220. Acts 2:22-36; 4:10-12; Rom 1:3-4.
221. Rom 3:25-26; 5:9; Heb 10:10.
222. Rom 3:27; 1 Cor 1:29-31; Gal 6:14; Eph 2:9; Phil 3:7-9.
223. Col 1:20; Heb 7:25; 9:12-14; 1 John 1:7.
224. Matt 26:28; Luke 24:47; Acts 10:43; Col 1:14.
225. Jer 31:33; Ezek 36:26-27; Eph 2:8-9; Phil 1:29.
226. John 3:16; 5:24; 6:40; Acts 13:48; Rom 5:21; 6:23; 1 Tim 1:16.
227. 1 Cor 2:21-23; Eph 1:3; 1 Pet 1:3.
228. Acts 4:12; Heb 7:27; 9:26.

means of reconciliation with God.[229] There is no other mediator between God and man than our Savior, Jesus Christ,[230] and he will receive with redeeming love all who come to him in faith.[231]

The Exaltation of Christ in His Saving Work

The exaltation of Christ in his resurrection, ascension, and reign reveals the full glory of his mediatorial work.[232] Raised by the power of God,[233] Christ triumphed over sin, death, and Satan,[234] and, as the firstfruits of the new creation,[235] gives eternal life to all who are united to him by faith.[236] Having ascended to the Father's right hand,[237] Christ pours out the Spirit on his people[238] and intercedes on their behalf[239] as a Great High Priest,[240] constantly advocating their cause[241] and granting them access into God's presence.[242] As the exalted Lord, Christ reigns with all authority as universal king[243] and head of his church,[244] governing the affairs of men and nations[245] and empowering his people to be victorious over sin and Satan.[246] The

229. Matt 28:19-20; Luke 24:47; Acts 17:30; Rom 10:14-17; 15:20.
230. 1 Tim 2:5.
231. Matt 11:28; John 6:37; Rev 5:9.
232. Eph 1:20-24; Col 1:18-20; Rev 5:5-14.
233. Acts 2:24; Rom 1:3-4.
234. John 12:31; Eph 1:20-21; Col 2:13-15; Heb 2:14-15.
235. 1 Cor 15:20, 23.
236. John 5:21; 6:40, 54; 1 Cor 15:45.
237. Acts 1:9; 2:33; Eph 4:8.
238. John 3:34; Acts 2:33.
239. Rom 8:34; Heb 7:25.
240. Heb 4:14-15.
241. 1 John 2:1.
242. Rom 5:2; Eph 2:18; 3:12.
243. Matt 28:18; Eph 1:22.
244. Eph 1:22; 5:23; Col 1:18.
245. Rev 1:5; 17:14; 19:16.
246. Eph 6:10-11; 1 John 5:4-5.

consummation of Christ's saving work will occur when he returns to judge the world in righteousness,[247] deliver the kingdom to his Father,[248] and receive eternal worship as King of kings and Lord of lords.[249]

---

247. Acts 17:31; Rom 2:16; 2 Tim 4:1.
248. 1 Cor 15:24.
249. Rev 17:14; 19:16.

THE PERSON AND
WORK OF THE HOLY SPIRIT

The Person of the Holy Spirit

The Holy Spirit is the third person[250] of the Trinity, who proceeds eternally from the Father[251] and the Son.[252] He is equal in deity, attributes, and nature with the Father and the Son,[253] and with them is to be worshipped and glorified. The Spirit manifests God's active presence in the world, giving life in God's creation[254] and new creation.[255] Existing forever with the Father and the Son, the Spirit is the agent of all blessing to God's creatures and makes possible communion with him.

---

250. Scripture teaches that would-be followers of Christ ought to be "[baptized] in the name of the Father and of the Son and of the Holy Spirit" (Matt 28:19), which implies the equal authority and dignity of the name of the Holy Spirit, which represents his person. Moreover, Scripture consistently attributes to the Spirit characteristics and activities that properly belong to a person, e.g., Isa 63:10; Matt 12:24; Luke 12:12; John 14:26; Acts 5:3-4, 9; 7:59; 13:2-4; 20:28; Eph 4:30; 2 Cor 3:17-18.

251. Prov 1:23; Isa 42:1; Luke 11:13; John 14:16-17, 26; 15:26; 1 Cor 2:10-12; Gal 3:5; 1 John 3:24.

252. John 5:21; cf. John 6:63; 15:26; 16:7, 13-15; Acts 2:17-18, 33; Rom 8:9-11; Gal 4:6; 1 Pet 1:11; John 15:26.

253. Lev 11:45; cf. Ps 51:11; 19:2; 139:7; 143:10; Isa 40:13-14; 63:1-11; Mic 3:8; Mark 10:18. See also Neh 9:20; Acts 1:8; Rom 1:4; 1 Cor 2:10-11; Titus 3:5; Heb 9:14; Rev 4:8.

254. Gen 2:7; 6:3; Job 33:4; 34:14-15.

255. John 3:1-15; 6:63; 7:37-39; Rom 8:11.

The Work of the Spirit Prior to Christ's Coming

The eternal Spirit was present at the beginning of God's creation,[256] carrying out the creative word of God[257] and giving life[258] to all things. In God's work under the old covenant, the Spirit was present with God's people[259] to consecrate, deliver, guide, and grant saving faith in the promises of God.[260] He empowered prophets to reveal God's Word,[261] appointed elders to render judgment,[262] raised up judges to bring deliverance,[263] anointed priests and kings as his representatives, and inspired the record of old covenant revelation.[264] Through all the institutions and offices of the Old Testament, the Spirit's work pointed to the ultimate revelation of God through his Son, Jesus Christ.[265]

The Work of the Spirit in Christ and the New Covenant

The Spirit's work in the new covenant centers on Christ and the church. It is by the Spirit that Jesus Christ was conceived and born of a virgin,[266] anointed to fulfill his earthly ministry,[267] empowered to offer his life as a sacrifice,[268] and raised in resurrection power.[269] After Christ

---

256. Gen 1:2.

257. Ps 33:6, 9; 104:30.

258. Job 33:4; 34:14-15; cf. Isa 32:14-17.

259. Deut 32:11-12 (cf. Isa 31:5; Gen 1:2); Ps 51:10-12; Isa 63:7-13; Hag 2:5; Zech 4:6.

260. Gen 15:6; cf. Gal 3:5-6; Heb 11:8-10.

261. Matt 22:43; Acts 1:16; 2 Pet 1:21.

262. Num 11:16-17, 25.

263. Judg 3:9-10; 6:34; 11:29; 13:24-25; 15:14.

264. 1 Sam 10:9; 16:13; 2 Chron 24:20; 2 Tim 3:16.

265. Heb 1:1-2; 7:23-24; 9:12; Matt 5:17-18; Mark 7:18-19; Luke 24:27; John 2:19, 21; 4:21, 23; 5:39, 46; Rom 10:4; 2 Cor 1:20.

266. Matt 1:18-20; Luke 1:35.

267. Isa 11:1-3; 61:1; Matt 3:16; 12:28-32; Mark 1:10; Luke 3:22; 4:16-21; John 1:32-34; Acts 1:2; 10:38; Heb 2:4.

268. Heb 9:14-15.

269. Rom 1:4; 8:11; 1 Pet 3:18-20.

ascended to the Father's right hand, the promised Holy Spirit descended at Pentecost and ushered in the new era of the Spirit's fullness,[270] indwelling believers and empowering them for life and service.[271] The Spirit glorifies Christ and bears witness to him, convicting the world concerning sin, righteousness, and judgment.[272] He inspired the record of new covenant revelation[273] and makes it effective in people's hearts through the gift of regeneration.[274] He illuminates God's Word to his people,[275] assures them of God's love,[276] comforts them with his presence,[277] intercedes on their behalf,[278] and sanctifies them in conformity to the image of Christ.[279] The Spirit is the bond of our union with Christ,[280] the seal of our salvation,[281] the firstfruits of our redemption,[282] and the guarantee of our inheritance.[283]

---

270. John 14:2-4, 16, 25-26; 16:5-7; Acts 1:4, 8; 2:1-4, 16-21, 33.

271. Luke 4:16-21; John 6:63; 16:13-14; Acts 1:8; 2:17-21; 1 Cor 12-14; Rom 14:17; 1 Tim 4:14; 1 Thess 5:19-21.

272. John 16:8-11.

273. John 14:17, 26; 16:13-15; 1 Cor 2:10-13; 2 Tim 3:16-17; 2 Pet 3:15-16; 1 Tim 5:18; cf. Luke 10:7; Matt 10:10; Deut 25:4.

274. John 3:5-8; Titus 3:5.

275. Eph 1:17-18; 1 Cor 2:12-14.

276. Rom 5:5; Gal 4:6; Eph 3:16-19.

277. John 16:7; Acts 9:31; 2 Cor 3:17-18; 13:14.

278. Rom 8:26-27; John 16:7.

279. Rom 8:13; 2 Cor 3:18; Gal 5:22-23.

280. Eph 4:3; 1 Cor 12:12-13; Gal 4:6.

281. 2 Cor 1:21-22; Eph 1:13; 4:30.

282. Rom 8:23; 1 Cor 15:20, 23.

283. Eph 1:13-14; cf. 2 Cor 1:22; 5:5.

THE GOSPEL AND THE APPLICATION
OF SALVATION
BY THE HOLY SPIRIT

The Gospel

The gospel is the good news of Jesus Christ and all that he did in his life, death, resurrection, and ascension to accomplish salvation for humanity.[284] Therefore, the gospel is not a human action or achievement but rather an objective, historical, divine achievement[285] that remains true and unchanging regardless of human opinion or response. The gospel stands as the core message of the Bible, which in all its parts testifies to God's saving acts culminating in the person and work of Christ.[286] This good news is the power of God for salvation for all who believe,[287] providing hope for the lost[288] and abiding comfort and strength for the believer.[289] There is no salvation apart from Jesus Christ, for there is no other name given under heaven by which we must be saved.[290]

---

284. Rom 3:23-26; 1 Cor 15:3-5; Rev 1:5; 5:5, 9-12.
285. Rom 1:3-4; 1 Cor 15:3-5.
286. Luke 24:44-47; John 5:39; 1 Pet 1:10-12.
287. Rom 1:16.
288. Matt 4:16; Acts 4:12; Rom 1:16.
289. Rom 5:1-5; 8:31-39; 2 Cor 1:3-5.
290. Acts 4:12.

God commands the gospel to be proclaimed to all people everywhere,[291] but all people are spiritually dead and unable to respond to this saving news.[292] Therefore, God graciously and effectually calls to himself those he chose to save in Christ.[293] Through the proclamation of the gospel, the Holy Spirit regenerates the elect and brings them into a living union with Christ, bestowing new spiritual life,[294] opening their eyes to see God's glory in Christ,[295] and enabling them to respond to the gospel in faith and repentance.[296] With a renewed heart and mind,[297] we receive Christ and rely fully on him for salvation, turning from our sinful, self-seeking way of life to love and follow Christ in joyful obedience.[298] Only those who respond to the gospel in this way will be saved,[299] yet even this response is a gift of God's merciful grace, ensuring that he alone receives the glory for our salvation.[300]

Justification and Adoption

In their union with Christ, believers freely receive all the benefits of the gospel.[301] Those whom God effectually calls to himself, he justifies in Christ,[302] forgiving all of

---

291. Matt 28:19-20; Luke 24:47; Acts 17:30; Rom 10:14-17; 15:20.
292. John 6:44; Eph 2:1-3, Col 2:13.
293. Rom 8:30; 1 Cor 1:24; Eph 4:4.
294. John 3:5-6, 8; 6:63; 2 Cor 3:6; Rom 10:14-17; Titus 3:5..
295. John 16:13-14; 2 Cor 3:16-18; 4:4, 6.
296. Eph 2:8-9; Phil 1:29.
297. Rom 12:2; 1 Cor 2:16; Eph 4:23.
298. 1 Thess 1:9.
299. Acts 4:12; Col 1:23.
300. Eph 2:8-9; Phil 1:29; 1 Cor 1:26-29.
301. Eph 1:3.
302. Rom 8:29-30.

their sins[303] and declaring them righteous and acceptable in his sight.[304] This declaration is judicial, addressing not our nature but our status with regard to God's law;[305] it is definitive, being neither gradually gained nor able to be lost;[306] and it is gracious, a free gift of God's righteousness based on nothing worked in us or by us, but received freely by faith.[307] The sole ground of our justification is the righteousness of Christ, whose life of perfect obedience is imputed to us and whose substitutionary death on our behalf completely satisfies the demands of God's justice toward our sins.[308] Those whom God justifies, he adopts into his family, granting them the full status, rights, and privileges of beloved sons.[309] As God's children, we receive his name,[310] enjoy access into his presence,[311] experience his care and discipline,[312] and eagerly await the glorious inheritance he promises his own.[313]

---

303. Rom 4:7; Col 1:14; Heb 8:12.

304. Rom 3:26; 5:19; 2 Cor 5:21.

305. Acts 13:39; Rom 3:26; 8:1-2.

306. Rom 3:28; 4:6.

307. Rom 3:22-26; 5:15-17; 1 Cor 1:29; Eph 2:8-9.

308. Rom 3:22-26; 1 Cor 1:29; 2 Cor 5:21; Eph 2:8-9.

309. Rom 8:15, 23; Gal 4:4-7; Eph 1:5; 1 John 3:1-2.

310. Num 6:27 (cf. Matt 28:19); Deut 28:10; 2 Chron 7:14; Acts 11:26; 2 Tim 2:19; 1 Pet 4:14, 16.

311. Rom 5:2; Eph 1:18.

312. Heb 12:5-11.

313. Rom 8:23-26; 1 Pet 1:3-5.

As the all-sufficient Savior, Christ also sanctifies his people, cleansing them from the impurity of sin and setting them apart for God and his service.[314] The renewing work of the Holy Spirit breaks their bondage to sin and Satan and raises them to new life, enabling believers to put sin to death and grow in likeness to Christ.[315] Sanctification is therefore both a definitive act of God[316] and a progressive work of the Spirit.[317] Believers must persevere in faith and obedience in order to be saved.[318] Yet this perseverance is also a gift of God in Christ, who preserves his own and keeps them safe forever.[319] The ultimate goal of sanctification is our full conformity to Christ's image, which will finally come when believers are raised physically with Christ in glory, freed from sin and exulting in the presence of God forever.[320]

314. 1 Cor 1:30; Eph 5:25-26; Heb 10:10, 14.

315. Rom 6:6-7, 18; 7:6; 8:12-13; Gal 5:1.

316. Heb 10:10, 14.

317. 2 Cor 7:1; Phil 2:12; 1 Tim 6:11; 2 Tim 2:22; Heb 12:14.

318. Matt 10:22; 24:13; Mark 13:13; Col 1:23; Heb 3:14.

319. Rom 8:29-30; 1 Cor 1:8; 1 Thess 3:13; 1 Pet 1:5; Jude 24.

320. Rom 8:29; 2 Cor 3:18; 1 John 3:1-3.

THE EMPOWERING
MINISTRY OF THE SPIRIT

The Filling of the Spirit

When Christ ascended, he poured out the Holy Spirit on the church, ushering in a greater experience of God's presence and power among his people.[321] The Spirit transforms hearts by the miracle of regeneration[322] and indwells all believers in abundant, new covenant measure.[323] The Spirit also desires to fill God's people continually with increased power for Christian life and witness.[324] To be filled with the Spirit is to be more fully under his influence,[325] more aware of his presence,[326] and more effective in his service.[327] All Christians, therefore, must continually seek to be filled with the Spirit[328] by living and praying in such a way that invites the Spirit's work among us, actively longing for God to accomplish his gracious purposes in us and through us.

---

321. Acts 2:17-18; 2:33; 10:45.

322. Titus 3:5; John 3:3; 1 Pet 1:3.

323. Ezek 36:26-27; Acts 2:38-39; 1 Cor 12:12-13.

324. Acts 1:8; 4:8; 4:31; 13:9; Eph 5:18.

325. Acts 2:42-47; 4:32-33.

326. Acts 3:19; 7:55; 19:6; Rom 8:15, 23.

327. Acts 4:8; 6:3.

328. Eph 5:18.

The filling of the Spirit brings to God's people a deeper knowledge of Christ,[329] an increased desire for holiness,[330] a stronger commitment to unity and love, a greater fruitfulness in ministry, and a deeper gratitude for our salvation.[331]

The Gifts of the Spirit

Christ loves the church, his body, and provides for its health and growth through the Holy Spirit.[332] In addition to giving new life, the Spirit sovereignly bestows gifts on every believer.[333] Spiritual gifts are those abilities and expressions of God's power given by his grace for the glory of Christ and the building up of the church.[334] The variety of these gifts—some permanent and some occasional, some more natural and some more remarkable—reflects[335] the diversity of the members of Christ's body[336] and demonstrates our need for one another.[337] The gifts are not to be exercised with apprehension, pride, or disorder, but with faith, love, and order,[338] and always in submission to the authority of Scripture as the final revelation of God.[339] With the exception of those among the apostles who were commissioned as eyewitnesses of Christ and made recipients of normative revelation,[340] the full range of spiritual gifts remain at work in the church and are given

329. John 15:26; 16:13-15; Eph 3:16-19; Rom 5:5.
330. Rom 8:13; Gal 5:22-23.
331. Rom 8:15-16; Eph 5:19-20; Col 1:11-14.
332. John 16:4-15; Eph 4:7-8, 13-16; 5:25-27.
333. 1 Cor 12:7, 11.
334. 1 Cor 12:7; 14:26; Eph 4:12.
335. Rom 12:6-8; 1 Cor 12:4-11, 28-30; 1 Pet 4:10-11; Eph 4:11-12.
336. 1 Cor 12:21-26.
337. 1 Cor 14:1; 13:1-3; 14:33.
338. 1 Cor 13:1-3, 14:1; 14:33.
339. 1 Thess 5:19-21; 1 Cor 14:29; 2 Tim 3:16; Rev 22:18-19.
340. Acts 1:20-26; John 14:26; 15:27; 16:13-15; 1 Cor 14:37; Gal 1:11-20; Rev 21:14.

for the good of the church and its witness to the world. We are therefore to earnestly desire and practice them until Christ returns.[341]

341. 1 Cor 1:7; 12:31; 13:8-12; 14:1, 12.

LIFE IN CHRIST

Growing in Christ

All believers, by virtue of their union with Christ, are progressively transformed into his image.[342] Although the ruling power of sin in our lives has been broken, remnants of corruption remain in our hearts that we will fight throughout our lives.[343] This lifelong process of growth takes place as the Spirit empowers us to abide in Christ and strive for holiness in every area of life.[344] Resting in Christ's finished work never renders our effort unnecessary but rather enables the joyful pursuit of loving and pleasing God.[345] Compelled by grace, believers grow in the knowledge of God, obey Christ's commands, walk by the Spirit, mortify sin, and pursue God's priorities and purposes.[346] Although such actions are not the ground of our salvation, they demonstrate the authenticity of our salvation and are a means by which God keeps us faithful

---

342. Rom 6:5-11; 2 Cor 3:18; Rev 19:8.

343. Gal 5:16-18; 1 Pet 2:11.

344. John 15:4-8; Gal 5:16-26; Heb 12:14.

345. Ps 37:5, 40:8; John 15:11; Rom 6:1-4; 12:1-2; Eph 5:10; Phil 1:25; Titus 2:11-14; 1 Pet 1:13-19.

346. Mark 12:30-31; John 15:10; Rom 8:4; 1 Cor 10:31; 2 Cor 4:6; Col 3:5-6; 1 John 5:2-3.

to the end.[347] Among the many public and private means of grace, the Word of God, prayer, and fellowship are primary instruments of our sanctification,[348] fostering communion with God and training us together to glorify him, love others, and testify to Christ in the world.[349]

Waiting for Christ

Living the Christian life involves longing[350] and waiting for the return of the Lord Jesus Christ.[351] Although believers are new creations in Christ and presently enjoy the blessings of his resurrection power,[352] their sanctification remains partial and incomplete in this life.[353] Furthermore, they continue to live in mortal bodies in a creation subject to futility,[354] opposed by the world,[355] the flesh,[356] and the devil.[357] The Word of God assures us that we are his beloved children,[358] yet such an assurance does not remove the reality of suffering, sorrow, and persecution in this present age.[359] The gospel enables us to rejoice in the midst of tribulations,[360] assured that his purposes are working for our good even in circumstances we do not understand.[361] Fixing our eyes on

---

347. Matt 25:31-46; Eph 2:8-10; Heb 3:12-14; 6:9-12; 10:19-27.

348. John 6:63; 17:17; Acts 2:42; Eph 4:15; 6:18; Col 3:16; 1 Thess 2:13-14; 2 Tim 3:16-17; Jude 20-21.

349. Matt 5:8; 1 Cor 10:31; Col 3:12-14; 1 Pet 2:9-12.

350. Rom 8:19, 23, 36; 1 Cor 16:22; 2 Cor 5:2.

351. Titus 2:13; Jude 21; Rev 22:20.

352. John 5:24; 6:47; Rom 6:2-5; 2 Cor 5:17; Eph 1:19-20.

353. Phil 3:12; 1 Thess 5:23; 1 John 1:8; 3:2.

354. Eccles 3:11, 14; Rom 8:20-23; 2 Cor 5:1-4; 1 Cor 15:53.

355. 1 John 2:16; 5:19.

356. Gal 5:17.

357. Eph 6:10-12; Jas 4:7; 1 Pet 5:8-9.

358. Rom 8:17; Gal 4:5-6; 1 John 3:2.

359. John 16:33; Acts 14:22; Rom 8:36; 1 Pet 3:14, 17; 4:19.

360. Rom 5:3; 8:23; 12:12; 2 Cor 5:2, 4; Col 1:24; 1 Pet 4:13.

361. Isa 43:1-3; Lam 3:21-24; Rom 8:28; Phil 1:6.

Jesus, we endure in faith and abound in hope,[362] confident that a day is fast approaching when sin and sorrow will be no more.[363]

362. Rom 12:12; 15:13; 2 Cor 1:6; 2 Tim 2:12; Heb 12:1-3; 1 Pet 2:19-20.
363. Isa 25:8; 35:10; 51:11; Rev 7:17; 21:4.

THE CHURCH OF CHRIST

The Universal Church

The universal church is the true, worshipping community of God's people, composed of all the elect from all time.[364] Throughout salvation history, God by his Word and Spirit has been calling sinful people out of the whole human race to create a new redeemed humanity,[365] whom Christ purchased with his blood.[366] With the giving of the Spirit at Pentecost,[367] God's people were reconstituted as his new covenant church,[368] in continuity with the old covenant people of God but now brought to fulfillment by the work of Christ.[369] All of God's people are united in one body[370]—with Christ as the supreme, sustaining, and life-giving head[371]— and set apart for God's own possession and purposes.[372]

---

364. Heb 12:22-23; 2:12; Eph 5:25; Rev 21:2.
365. Gen 12:1-3; Exod 6:7; 19:3-6; Deut 4:10; Eph 2:11-22; Col 1:13.
366. Acts 20:28; Eph 1:7; 5:25.
367. Acts 2:1-4.
368. Acts 2:42-47.
369. Jer 31:31-33; Rom 11:25; Eph 1:23, 2:13-22; 3:6; Heb 8:8-10.
370. Eph 4:4-6; 1 Cor 12:12-27.
371. Col 1:18; 2:19; Eph 1:22-23; 4:15-16; 5:23.
372. 1 Pet 2:9-10; Lev 19:2.

As an expression of Christ's universal church, the local church is the focal point of God's plan to mature his people and save sinners.[373] Therefore, all Christians are to join themselves as committed members to a specific local church.[374] A true church is marked by the faithful preaching of the Word,[375] the right administration of the sacraments,[376] and the proper exercise of church discipline.[377] Even true churches are imperfect: they often contain a mixture of unbelievers hidden among the true flock[378] and are vulnerable to theological error and moral failure.[379] Yet Christ is unwavering in his commitment to build his church and will surely bring it to maturity.[380]

Christ has given the offices of elder[381] and deacon[382] to the church.[383] Elders occupy the sole office of governance and are called to teach, oversee, care for, and protect the flock entrusted to them by the Lord.[384] Deacons provide for the various needs of the church through acts of service. God gives these and other people as gifts to serve and equip the saints for the work of ministry, for building up the body of Christ.[385] In keeping with God's created design Scripture

373. Eph 3:10; 1 Tim 3:15; Matt 28:18-20.

374. Acts 2:47; 1 Cor 1:2; 1 Thess 1:1.

375. 2 Tim 2:15; 2 Tim 4:1-2; Titus 1:9.

376. Matt 28:19; Acts 2:38; Rom 6:3-4; Matt 26:26-28; 1 Cor 11:17-34.

377. Matt 18:15-17; 1 Cor 5:1-13.

378. 2 Tim 2:16-19; Acts 20:29-30; 2 Tim 4:10.

379. 1 Cor 3:1-3; 5:1; 1 Tim 5:20; 2 Tim 4:3-4; Rev 2:5, 14-16, 20-23; 3:2-3, 15-19.

380. Matt 16:18; Eph 5:25-27; Rev 19:7-9.

381. 1 Tim 3:1-7; Titus 1:5-9; Acts 14:23; 20:28; 1 Tim 5:17-18; Heb 13:17.

382. 1 Tim 3:8-13; Phil 1:1.

383. Eph 4:11-12; 1 Cor 12:28.

384. 1 Pet 5:1-4; Acts 20:28; 1 Tim 3:2; 2 Tim 4:1-2; 1 Tim 5:17.

385. Eph 4:11-12.

reserves the office of elder for men,[386] yet men and women alike belong to a royal priesthood in which each member is gifted by God to play a vital role in the life and mission of the church.[387]

The Sacraments of the Church

The sacraments are precious means of grace that signify the benefits of the gospel, confirm its promises to the believer, and visibly distinguish the church from the world.[388] The Lord Jesus instituted two sacraments, baptism and the Lord's Supper,[389] for faithful observance by the church[390] until his return.[391] Baptism is an initiatory, unrepeated sacrament[392] for those who come to faith in Christ that pictures their remission of sins and union with Christ in his death and resurrection.[393] Through immersion in water in the name of the Father, Son, and Holy Spirit,[394] the believer publicly proclaims his faith in Christ and signifies his entrance into the body of Christ.[395] Although commanded by Christ and a true means of grace, grace is not so inseparably tied to baptism that no one can be saved without it, or that everyone who is baptized is thereby saved.[396]

---

386. 1 Tim 2:12-13.

387. Rom 16:1-16; Acts 1:14; 9:36-42; 16:14-15; 18:2; Phil 4:2-3; 1 Tim 5:9-16; 2 Tim 1:5; Titus 2:1-6; 1 Pet 2:9.

388. Rom 4:11; cf. Gen 17:7; Rom 6:3-4; 1 Cor 10:16-20; Gal 3:26-28; Col 2:11-14.

389. Matt 28:19; 1 Cor 11:23-26; cf. Matt 26:26-29; Mark 14:22-25; Luke 22:14-23.

390. Acts 2:42-46.

391. Matt 28:20; 1 Cor 11:26.

392. Acts 2:38-41; Gal 2:16; 3:26-27; 5:2-6; cf. Col 2:11-14.

393. Rom 6:3-5.

394. Matt 28:19; Acts 19:3-5.

395. Acts 22:16; Rom 6:3-14; Col 2:11-14.

396. 1 Cor 10:1-5; 1 Pet 3:21; Rom 2:28; cf. Col 2:11-14.

In the Lord's Supper, the gathered church eats bread, signifying Christ's body given for his people, and drinks the cup of the Lord, signifying his blood shed for our sins.[397] As we observe this sacrament with faith and sober self-examination,[398] we remember and proclaim the death of Christ, commune with him and receive spiritual nourishment for our souls, signify our unity with other members of Christ's body, and look forward to the Lord's triumphant return.[399]

The Purpose and Mission of the Church

As the body of Christ, the church exists to worship God,[400] to edify and mature his people,[401] and to bear witness to Christ and his kingdom in all the world.[402] Governed by Scripture, the church gathers for the teaching of the Word,[403] prayer, [404] the sacraments,[405] congregational singing,[406] fellowship, and mutual edification through the exercise of spiritual gifts.[407] As the Father sent Jesus into the world, so Jesus has sent his people into the world in the power of the Spirit.[408] The church's mission is to make disciples of all nations, teaching them to observe all that Christ has commanded.[409] We do this by proclaiming the gospel, planting churches,

---

397. 1 Cor 11:23-26.
398. 1 Cor 11:26-30.
399. 1 Cor 11:26.
400. Col 3:16; Eph 5:18-20.
401. Eph 4:12-13; Col 1:28.
402. Matt 28:19.
403. 2 Tim 4:1-2; 1 Tim 4:13; Eph 4:11-12.
404. Acts 2:42; 1 Tim 2:1-2.
405. Rom 6:3-4; 1 Cor 11:17-34.
406. Col 3:16; Eph 5:18-20.
407. 1 Cor 12:7; 14:26; 1 Thess 5:11; 1 Pet 4:10.
408. John 17:18; 20:21; Luke 24:44-49; Acts 1:5-8.
409. Matt 28:18-20.

and adorning the proclamation of the gospel through our love and good works. There will always be a gathering of believers on earth because the Lord promises to build, guide, and preserve his church to the end of the age.[410] When Christ returns, he will gather and perfect his church from every tribe, tongue, and nation as a people for his own possession, and he will dwell with them forever.[411]

410. Matt 16:18.
411. 1 Thess 4:16-17; 1 John 3:2; 1 Cor 15:51-52; 2 Cor 5:1; Titus 2:13-14; Rev 7:13-17; 19:6-9; 21:1-4.

THE LAST THINGS

Death and the Intermediate State

Death entered God's good creation as a result of Adam's sin, and now all people are subject to God's curse of death.[412] Yet believers have no need to fear,[413] because Christ has conquered death and delivered us from its dominion.[414] Although our bodies return to dust for a time,[415] death for the Christian has become a doorway to paradise,[416] where our souls enter immediately into God's presence[417] to behold and enjoy our Savior and to rest from our labors.[418] In company with all the spirits of the righteous made perfect,[419] we will await the redemption of our bodies[420] and our full and final salvation.[421] The souls of the unredeemed,

412. Gen 3:17-19; Rom 5:12; 6:23.

413. 1 Cor 15:56-57; 1 Thess 4:13; Heb 2:14-15.

414. John 11:25-26; Rom 6:8-9; Gal 3:13-14; Heb 2:14-15; Rev 5:5-6; 21:4.

415. Gen 3:19.

416. Luke 23:43.

417. Eccles 12:7; 2 Cor 5:6-8; Phil 1:23; Rev 6:9-11.

418. Ps 16:11; John 17:24; Phil 1:21-23; Rev 14:13.

419. Heb 12:23.

420. Rom 8:23.

421. Matt 25:31-36; Rev 6:10-11.

however, are cast immediately into hades to experience torment[422] as they await final judgment for their sins.[423]

Christ's Return and the Resurrection

At the appointed time known only to God,[424] Jesus Christ will return to the earth in power and glory[425] as Judge[426] and King[427] to whom every knee will bow.[428] Christ's personal,[429] physical,[430] and visible[431] return is the blessed hope of all who trust in him.[432] At the end of the age the just and the unjust will be raised as their souls are reunited to their bodies: the just to a resurrection of life, the unjust to a resurrection of judgment.[433] When the dead in Christ are raised,[434] their perishable bodies will be redeemed and made like Christ's imperishable, glorious, powerful, spiritual body.[435] Those in Christ who are alive shall likewise be changed,[436] and thus will all God's glorified people forever bear the image of their Savior.[437]

422. Luke 16:23-24; Rev 20:13.
423. Matt 25:31-33, 41-43.
424. Matt 24:36, 44; Mark 13:33; 1 Thess 5:2-3.
425. Luke 21:27.
426. Ps 96:10-13; Isa 11:1-5; John 5:26-29; 2 Tim 4:1.
427. Rev 19:11-16.
428. Phil 2:9-11.
429. Acts 1:9-11; 1 Thess 4:16.
430. Luke 24:39-43; Acts 1:11; Phil 3:20-21.
431. Mark 14:61-62; Matt 24:26-27; Rev 1:7.
432. Titus 2:13.
433. John 5:28-29; Acts 24:15; 2 Cor 5:2-4.
434. 1 Cor 15:51-52; 1 Thess 4:15-17.
435. Rom 8:23-24; 1 Cor 15:42-49, 53; Phil 3:21; 1 John 3:2.
436. 1 Cor 15:49-53; 1 Thess 4:15-17.
437. 1 Cor 15:49.

On the last day all people will appear before Christ, who is the judge of all.[438] Those who suppressed God's truth in unrighteousness and did not obey the gospel of Christ [439] will suffer the righteous wrath of God[440] and be justly cast into the hell of fire with the devil and his angels.[441] There they will experience eternal, conscious punishment according to their sins.[442] Those saved by Christ, whose names are written in the book of life, will be welcomed into the joy of their master and richly rewarded for every good work done in his name.[443] God's glorified people will inherit the kingdom[444] from which all sin, sorrow, suffering, and death will be banished.[445] Christ as king will set all of creation free from its bondage to corruption,[446] making new the heavens and the earth[447] and establishing his eternal rule in his consummated kingdom.[448] Surrounded by unimaginable beauty,[449] we will enjoy unhindered communion with our triune God,[450] beholding him, serving him, worshipping him, and reigning with him forever and ever.[451] Amen. Come, Lord Jesus!

---

438. Matt 25:31-32; Acts 17:30-31; Rom 14:12; 2 Cor 5:10; 2 Tim 4:1; Rev 20:11-15.

439. Rom 1:18-21; 2 Thess 1:8.

440. John 3:36; Rom 2:5; Eph 5:6; Rev 14:10, 19; 16:19; 19:15; 20:10.

441. Matt 5:22; 13:49-50; 25:41-46; Mark 9:43-48.

442. Luke 12:47-48; Rev 14:9-11; 20:10-13; 21:8.

443. Matt 10:42; 25:21-23, 31-40; 1 Cor 3:12-15; 4:5; Rev 20:12.

444. Matt 25:34; Eph 1:13-14; 1 Pet 1:3-5.

445. Rev 21:4, 27.

446. Rom 8:20-22.

447. Isa 65:17; 2 Pet 3:13; Rev 21:1, 5.

448. Matt 25:31; 1 Cor 15:24; Rev 22:1-3.

449. 1 Cor 2:9; Rev 21:9-13; 22:1-5.

450. Ps 16:11; Matt 25:35; Eph 2:6-7; Rev 21:3.

451. 1 John 3:2; 1 Thess 4:17; 2 Tim 2:12; Rev 3:21; 22:3-5.

Made in the USA
Las Vegas, NV
07 April 2024